Neil Armstrong
Meet the Famous Astronaut

Barbara Kramer

Enslow Publishers, Inc.

40 Industrial Road   PO Box 38
Box 398   Aldershot
Berkeley Heights, NJ 07922 Hants GU12 6BP
USA   UK

http://www.enslow.com

Library of Congress Cataloging-in-Publication Data

Kramer, Barbara.
   Neil Armstrong : meet the famous astronaut / by Barbara Kramer.
      p. cm. — (Meeting famous people)
   Summary: A biography of Neil Armstrong, whose childhood dreams of flying came true in 1969 when he became the first man to walk on the Moon.
   ISBN 0-7660-2007-X
   1. Armstrong, Neil, 1930—Juvenile literature. 2. Astronauts—United States—Biography—Juvenile literature. 3. Project Apollo—Juvenile literature. [1. Armstrong, Neil, 1930– 2. Astronauts. 3. Space flight to the Moon. 4. Project Apollo (U.S.)] I. Title. II. Series.
   TL789.85.A75S38 2003
   629.45'0092—dc21
                                               2003001725

Printed in the United States of America

10 9 8 7 6 5 4 3 2 1

To Our Readers: We have done our best to make sure all Internet Addresses in this book were active and appropriate when we went to press. However, the author and the publisher have no control over and assume no liability for the material available on those Internet sites or on other Web sites they may link to. Any comments or suggestions can be sent by e-mail to comments@enslow.com or to the address on the back cover.

Illustration Credits: National Aeronautics and Space Administration (NASA), pp. 3, 4, 8, 10, 12, 13, 15, 16, 17, 20, 23, 24, 25, 26, 29; Ohio Historical Society, pp. 6, 7, 11, 19.

Cover Illustrations: Courtesy of National Aeronautics and Space Administration

Table of Contents

Chapter 1

A Young Pilot

When Neil Armstrong was a boy, he kept having the same dream. In the dream, he could float just above his bed if he held his breath. He did not like that dream because he never went anywhere. Neil wanted to go places, and he would. In 1969, he made history as the first man to walk on the Moon.

Neil was born in his grandparents' house on August 5, 1930. They lived near the small town of

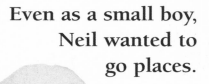

Wapakoneta, Ohio. Neil was the oldest of Stephen and Viola Armstrong's three children.

Neil's interest in flying began early. He went on his first airplane ride when he was six years old. He and his father rode in a small plane called the *Tin Goose*. The plane was noisy, and the wind made it bounce. Neil's father was scared. But Neil loved it.

Neil also enjoyed building model airplanes. As he got older, he built better planes with more detail. They also cost more. His parents said he needed to work for the things he wanted. So Neil got a job mowing grass. It was hard work. But it gave him money to buy supplies for his models.

Neil liked to do other things, too. He played the horn in the school band. He was also an *Eagle Scout*. But he never lost interest in flying.

Neil began flying lessons when he was fourteen. He paid for them by working at a drugstore. He stocked shelves, swept the floor, and helped customers. He earned forty cents an hour for his work. But it cost nine

Neil played with the school band.

dollars for each flying lesson. It took Neil a long time to save up enough money for even one lesson!

He got his pilot's license on his sixteenth birthday. He did not have a driver's license yet, but he could fly planes.

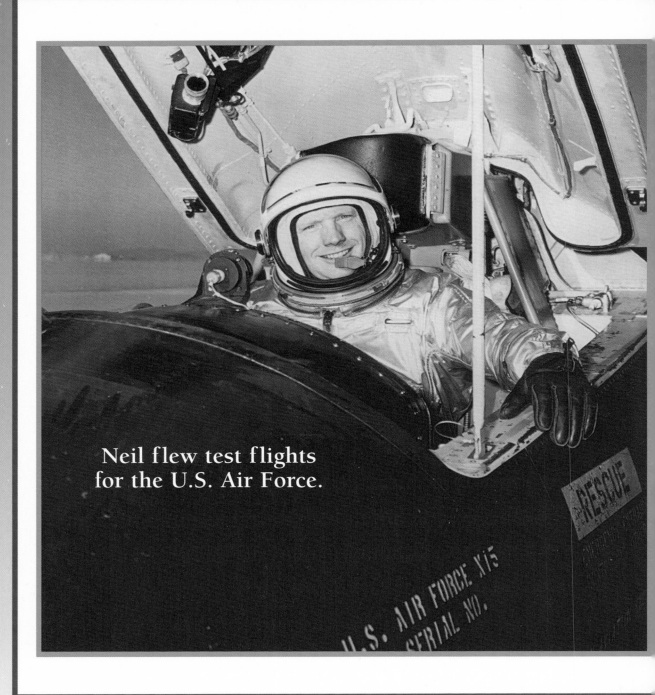

Neil flew test flights
for the U.S. Air Force.

Chapter 2

Flying Higher

Neil started college at Purdue University in 1947. He learned about flight and how airplanes are designed.

During his second year of college, he left school to join the Navy. He was twenty years old and the youngest pilot in his squadron. He soon earned his wings as a Navy fighter pilot.

At that time, the United States was fighting in the Korean War. In 1951, the Navy sent Neil to fight.

He flew missions to bomb bridges, trains, and tanks. He took off and landed on a special ship called an aircraft carrier. It was dangerous work. One time a wire tore part of a wing off Neil's plane. The enemy had strung the wire across a valley to keep out low-flying airplanes. Neil was able to keep the damaged plane in

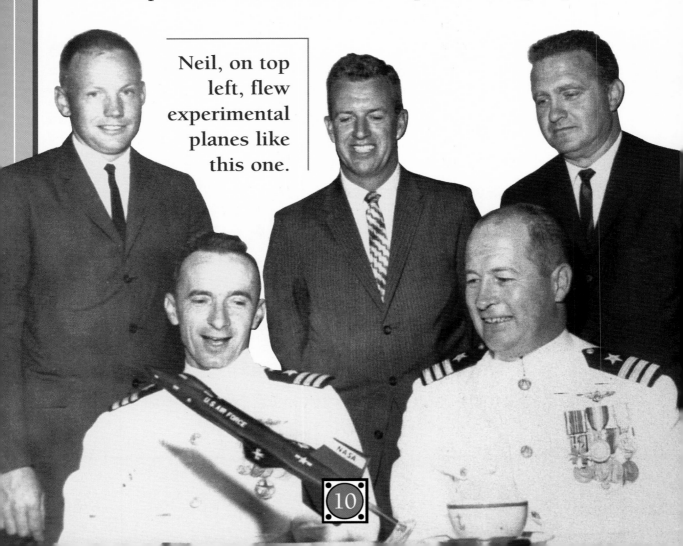

Neil, on top left, flew experimental planes like this one.

the air long enough to land safely on the aircraft carrier. Neil flew seventy-eight times on missions. He earned three medals for his bravery.

Neil's work with the Navy ended in 1952. He then went back to Purdue University.

He graduated from college in 1955. A year later, he married Janet Shearon, a student he met at Purdue. They moved to California where Neil got a job as a test pilot. He made flights in new jets to test them.

Janet Shearon married Neil in 1956.

In 1962, Neil signed up to become an astronaut. He wanted to fly into space. The first group of seven astronauts had already made the first space flights.

Neil trains in the lunar module simulator.

One of those astronauts, John Glenn, had circled the earth three times in his small Mercury space capsule. Americans were excited about the space program. They wanted their countrymen to be the first to land on the Moon.

This model shows how astronauts could land on the Moon.

After many tests, Neil was chosen as one of a second group of astronauts. He and his wife, Jan, and their young son, Eric, moved to Houston, Texas. Their second son, Mark, was born in Houston. Their only daughter, Karen, was born in 1959.

Neil trained as an astronaut at the Manned Spacecraft Center (renamed the Lyndon B. Johnson Space Center in 1973). He learned about space and the space vehicles he would be flying.

Finally, Neil was assigned to his first flight in space.

Chapter 3

Danger in Space

Neil was the command pilot for the *Gemini 8* mission. It meant that he would fly the spaceship. The other astronaut for that flight was David Scott. Their special job would be to dock, or hook up with, an unmanned spacecraft or satellite. It would be the first time two vehicles docked in space.

On March 16, 1966, *Gemini 8* shot off the launchpad in Cape Canaveral, Florida. The other spacecraft had been launched forty minutes earlier.

It took about five hours for *Gemini 8* to catch up with the spacecraft. Neil flew past it. Then he turned *Gemini 8* around to face the spacecraft.

He fired small engines called thrusters. They moved *Gemini 8* toward the satellite. Neil flew within 150 feet from the spacecraft for about thirty minutes. Both vehicles were traveling at about

Astronauts make their way to the *Gemini 8*.

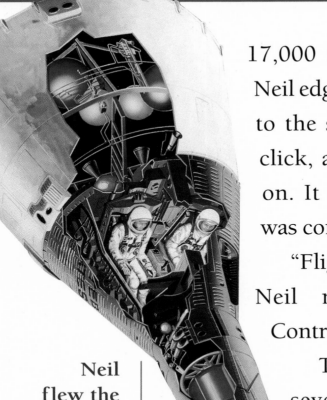

17,000 miles per hour. Then Neil edged *Gemini 8* even closer to the spacecraft. He heard a click, and a green light came on. It showed that *Gemini 8* was connected to the satellite.

"Flight, we are docked!" Neil reported to Mission Control.

Trouble started twenty-seven minutes after docking. The two vehicles, which were still linked together, began tumbling. Around and around they went. Neil undocked from the satellite. But *Gemini 8* rolled even faster. The sun and Earth alternately flashed by the windows with the *Gemini 8* completing a full turn every second.

Neil flew the *Gemini 8* capsule.

If the spinning did not stop, the astronauts would pass out. *Gemini 8* would break up.

But Neil and David stayed calm. They turned off all the main thrusters. There were other thrusters that were to be used to slow *Gemini 8* down when they came back to Earth. Neil fired those thrusters. It worked! *Gemini 8* stopped spinning.

Neil made an emergency splashdown in the Pacific Ocean.

Neil and David were awarded medals for the courage they showed during that space emergency.

Neil soon began training for his next trip into space.

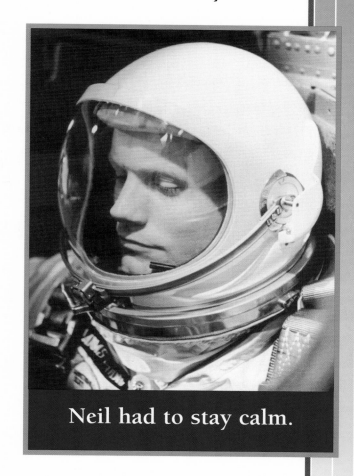

Neil had to stay calm.

Chapter 4

Man on the Moon

I n 1969, Neil learned that he would be the flight commander of the *Apollo 11* mission. That flight would be the first landing on the Moon. Two other astronauts were also chosen for that mission. They were Michael Collins and Edwin Aldrin, Jr., who was called Buzz.

The crew was awakened at 4:15 A.M. on July 16, 1969. After a breakfast of steak and eggs, they climbed into the *Apollo 11* spacecraft. It sat high on top of a huge Saturn V rocket that would blast them into space. Millions of people lined the beaches up and down the Florida coast to watch the launch. Millions more watched the countdown on their televisions.

". . . Four, three, two, one, zero, all engines running," said a voice on a loudspeaker.

The ground shook as the giant rocket rose off the launchpad in a cloud of fire and smoke. "Lift off! We have a lift off!"

The Armstrong family waits on Earth.

19

The *Apollo 11* Saturn V space vehicle lifts off.

The astronauts were on their way to the moon at 9:32 A.M.

It would take three days to get to the Moon. During those three days in transit, the astronauts were busy. They checked the equipment, and they broadcast television shows. People could watch at home as the astronauts showed them around the two spacecrafts that made up *Apollo 11*. The two spacecrafts were docked nose to nose so the crew could go from one to the other through hatches. The spacecrafts were filled with bundles of wiring and plumbing.

The larger of the two spacecrafts was named *Columbia*. That was where the astronauts spent most of their time. *Columbia* was not designed to land on the Moon. Neil and Buzz would travel to the Moon in the smaller vehicle, *Eagle*. Michael would stay in *Columbia* circling the Moon.

On July 19, the astronauts got their first close-up look at the Moon. The next day, Neil and Buzz climbed into the *Eagle* spacecraft. Michael pushed a button that sent *Eagle* on its way.

As they got close to the Moon, alarms sounded. *Eagle*'s computer could not keep up with all the information going through it.

"Go," said Mission Control. It meant that it was safe to go ahead with the landing.

But Neil saw another problem. *Eagle's* computer was taking them to a place on the Moon that had large craters and rocks. They had to land on flat ground. If the ship fell over or an engine hit a rock, they would be unable to take off again. The astronauts would die on the Moon.

Neil would have to land the spacecraft himself. There was not much time. *Eagle* was running out of landing fuel.

Neil quickly steered the vehicle to a flat spot. A light flashed on just before touchdown. "The *Eagle* has landed," Neil told Mission Control. *Eagle* had touched down on the Moon's surface.

The two astronauts were supposed to sleep, but they could not. They were too excited. After six and a half hours on the surface of the Moon, it was time for Neil and Buzz to explore. They put on their bulky

The lunar module, *Eagle*.

Neil's footprint on the Moon.

spacesuits. Then Neil opened *Eagle*'s hatch and started down the ladder.

There was a camera on the outside of *Eagle*. Six hundred million people on Earth watched Neil on television. He stepped three feet off the ladder and onto the Moon. "That's one small step for a man, one giant leap for mankind," he said.

Then Buzz joined Neil on the Moon's surface. They had a lot to do in the short time they would spend on the Moon.

They gathered soil samples and rocks to take back

to Earth. They also set up some experiments on the Moon. They raised an American flag, although it was not easy. The ground was as hard as concrete. Then they answered a telephone call from President Richard Nixon. He was calling all the way from Earth.

Neil and Edwin proudly display the American flag.

The astronauts spent about two and a half hours outside the *Eagle* on the Moon's surface. Then it was time to climb back into the spacecraft.

They could not leave the Moon right away. They had to wait until *Columbia* was in the right spot so that the two space vehicles could dock.

Earth as seen from the Moon.

Finally, that time came. They took off from the Moon and docked with *Columbia* four hours later. Neither had slept for almost forty hours. Then they started home.

Chapter 5

Splashdown!

The astronauts splashed down in the Pacific Ocean on July 24. But they had left two special things on the Moon. One was an American flag. The other was a message. It read: "HERE MEN FROM THE PLANET EARTH FIRST SET FOOT UPON THE MOON, JULY 1969 A.D. WE CAME IN PEACE FOR ALL MANKIND."

After their return the astronauts were honored with a parade in New York City.

Crowds gathered to see Neil, Edwin, and Michael during a Chicago parade.

Neil left the space program in 1971. He lived on a farm in Ohio and taught space science until 1978 at the University of Cincinnati. Later, he became a businessman. But Neil Armstrong will always be remembered best as the first man to walk on the Moon.

Timeline

1930~Born in Wapakoneta, Ohio, on August 5.

1947~Enters Purdue University.

1949~Begins training as a Navy fighter pilot.

1951~Sent to fight in the Korean War.

1952~Finishes his work with the Navy; returns to Purdue University.

1955~Graduates from college; becomes a test pilot.

1962~Becomes an astronaut.

1966~First space flight on *Gemini 8*.

1969~Becomes the first man to walk on the Moon; leaves the Presidential Medal of Freedom.

1971~Retires from the space program.

2002~Works as a businessman.

Words to Know

command pilot—Astronaut who flies a space vehicle.

engineer—A person trained in how engines and machines work and how to design them.

mission—A special job assigned by the people in charge.

Mission Control—An area responsible for the health and safety of a space crew and the successful accomplishment of mission goals.

satellite—Any object that circles, or orbits, another object. Man-made satellites are launched from Earth. They can be used to collect information from space, but they do not carry astronauts into space.

splashdown—The landing of a spacecraft in the ocean.

thrusters—Small engines on a spacecraft. They are used to move a vehicle up and down or to turn it right or left in space. Thrusters on the back of the spacecraft slow it down when the vehicle returns to Earth.

Learn More

Books

Brown, Don. *One Giant Leap: The Story of Neil Armstrong*. Boston: Houghton Mifflin Company, 1998.

Fraser, Mary Ann. *One Giant Leap*. New York: Henry Holt and Company, 1993.

Siy, Alexandra. *Footprints on the Moon*. Watertown, Mass.: Charlesbridge Publishing, 2001.

Suen, Anastasia. *Man on the Moon*. New York: The Penguin Group, 1997.

Internet Addresses

<http://www.hq.nasa.gov/office/pao/History/ap11ann/comments.htm>

<http://www.surfnetkids.com/space.htm>

<http://kids.msfc.nasa.gov>

Index